How to Handle Relationships Like an Adult

A practical guide for an effective and healthy relationship

Sherrie R. Salls

Copyright © 2023 [Sherrie R. Salls]

Disclaimer

The information provided in this book is for general purposes only. While every effort has been made to ensure the accuracy and completeness of the content, the author makes no representations or warranties, express or implied, regarding the suitability, applicability, or completeness of the information provided. The author shall not be responsible or liable for any loss, damage, or injury that may arise from the use or misuse of the information contained in this book.

About the author

Meet Sherrie Salls, the perceptive mind behind the game-changing book "How to Handle Relationships Like an Adult ". Sherrie has a great deal of experience and is passionate about creating lasting relationships, which gives her a unique viewpoint on the challenges of growing up in a partnership.

Sherrie R. Salls is an author, relationship specialist, and supporter of personal development. She is committed to enabling people to negotiate the complex dynamics of love and connection with maturity and intention. Through her personal experience and professional knowledge, Sherrie offers readers useful advice and doable tactics to improve their relationship-building game.

Sherrie's dedication to creating positive relationships is evident in her book, which skillfully blends advice, real-world examples, and a sympathetic grasp of human nature. Her writing is interesting, realistic, and intended to speak to readers at different points in their relationship journeys.

For those who are prepared to hange their relationships and approach love with a newfound maturity, Sherrie's book "How to Handle Relationships Like an Adult" is a must-read. Her expertise is evident whether you're looking for advice on confident boundary-setting, nurturing self-discovery, or effective communication.

Come along on this insightful trip with Sherrie R. Salls and allow her knowledge lead you into mature, satisfying relationships. Sherri inspires readers to embrace resilience, communication, and personal development in their search for deep relationships through her inspirational ideas. Prepare to manage your relationships as an adult and set out on a path to enduring, satisfying relationships.

Contents

Introduction

There is a story full of depth, development, and the nuanced interaction between "you" and "I" in the complex dance of relationships, where two souls entwine. This investigation delves deeply into the subtleties of managing a relationship, accepting the highs and lows, and realizing the rich tapestry that is created when two people set out on a common path of love and connection.

Think of "you" and "I" as notes in a melody that goes along with "us," rather than as two distinct entities in the emotional symphony that is a relationship. This trip explorer the depths of comprehension, communication, and the tenacious spirit that unites two hearts—it goes beyond the surface of romantic relationships.

Relationships are dynamic, breathing things that change with time; they are not static. We walks you through the ups and downs of preserving, growing, and living in the complex dynamics of "you" and "I" together. It's an invitation to see the tides of feelings, the dance of giving in, and the skill of creating a bond that endures the ages.

'You' and 'I' are both actively contributing to the story as we set out on this journey through the maze of connections. This trip is an investigation of dialogue, comprehension, and the strong ties that elevate a simple acquaintance into a meaningful collaboration.

This investigation should be more than just a contemplation; it should be an active dialogue between "you" and "I," delving into the depths of intimacy, enduring hardships, and savoring happy times. Come explores the layers of connections with us, as every interaction becomes a brushstroke in the masterpiece of our shared experiences and the dynamic story of "us."

Chapter 1. Building A Healthy Collaboration

Suggestions for Building a Good Relationship

Whether you're attempting to salvage a failed marriage or establish a new one, these tips will make you feel valued and connected by your partner.

building a healthy collaboration
Every romantic relationship has its ups and downs and calls for work, commitment, and a willingness to change and develop with your partner. Regardless of how long you've been dating or how recent your relationship is, there are steps you can take to build a healthy one. Even if you've had a lot of unsuccessful relationships in the past or have previously struggled to rekindle the love in your current relationship, you may find techniques to stay connected, achieve contentment, and enjoy long-lasting happiness.

What makes a partnership wholesome?

Relationships are formed for many different reasons, and each one is unique. One of the things that distinguishes a healthy relationship is having clear expectations for what you both want the partnership to become and go toward. Only by having open and honest discussions with your partner can you learn that.

However, most healthy relationships also have a few things in common. Notwithstanding the challenges or goals you both have, knowing these core principles will help you keep a fulfilling, intriguing, and meaningful relationship.

You two still share a strong emotional connection. You both make the other feel loved and emotionally fulfilled. Being and feeling loved are not the same things.
 When your spouse shows you love, you feel valued and accepted—almost as though they truly get you. Some relationships come to a peaceful cohabitation where there's no real emotional bond between the spouses. Even if the relationship could seem strong at first glance, a lack of ongoing involvement and emotional connections only serves to exacerbate the distance between the two people.

You're not afraid of civil discord. Some couples like to dispute quietly and loudly, while others may raise their voices to let the other know they disagree. However, not being afraid of conflict is the key to a happy marriage. You should be able to resolve conflicts without suffering humiliation or denigration, and you should be allowed to express your concerns without fear of repercussions.

Outside of work, you continue your relationships and pastimes. As romantic literature and films may suggest, no one can satisfy all of your desires. In actuality, having extremely high expectations for your partner can cause detrimental tension in a partnership. Sustaining your interests and hobbies, maintaining your identity outside of the partnership, and maintaining your relationships with family and friends are all essential for enhancing and energizing a romantic relationship.

You communicate openly and sincerely. Good communication is a prerequisite for all types of partnerships. When both partners are clear on what they want out of the relationship and feel comfortable communicating their wants, concerns, and desires, the link between you may grow and trust can be increased.

Chapter 2. The Difference Between Falling and Remaining in Love

The majority of individuals think that falling in love just happens. Maintaining that "falling in love" feeling—or staying in love—takes work and commitment. However, given the advantages, the effort is unquestionably valuable. A solid, healthy romantic relationship can improve all aspects of your welfare and be a continual source of joy and support in your life, both in good times and bad. You can protect or rekindle your romantic feelings today and build a lasting relationship that will last a lifetime.

Many couples focus their attention on their relationship only when there are specific, unavoidable problems to work through. People usually turn their attention back to their careers, family, or other pastimes once the concerns have been resolved. However, love requires ongoing attention and commitment to flourish in romantic relationships. As long as you think a love connection is important, you will have to invest time and attention into keeping it healthy. Moreover, resolving a small problem in your relationship today can often prevent it from growing into a much larger one down the road.

You can stay in that passionate connection and that state of being in love with the help of the following suggestions.

First tip: Take advantage of face-to-face time.

You fall in love as you look at each other and talk. If you continue to gaze and listen with the same level of attention, you might be able to sustain the sense of being in love for a very long period. You probably remember your early dating years with your lover in a positive light. Everything seemed new and exciting, and you were probably thinking of interesting new things to do or talking for hours on end. But as time goes on, the demands of family, jobs, and other responsibilities, together with our shared need for private time, may make it harder to find time for one another.

A common experience for couples is that their early exchanges of face-to-face contact gradually give way to hurried emails, texts, and instant chats. Digital communication has numerous uses, but it doesn't benefit the brain and nervous system in the same ways that face-to-face communication does. If you don't even take the time to sit down and chat with your spouse, they will still believe you don't understand or value them, even if you tell them you love them by text or voice message. In addition, you'll become more aloof or remote in a relationship. Regardless of how busy life may seem, you must make time for each other since face-to-face communication is the only way you can get the emotional cues required to feel valued……

Decide that you will get some quality time in regularly. Put your electronics away and stop worrying about anything else for some time each day to genuinely focus on and connect with your partner, regardless of how busy you are.

Pick an activity that the two of you like doing together, such as a daily stroll, dancing class, morning coffee, or a shared interest.

Try something new as a group. Taking part in new activities together helps keep people interested and promotes camaraderie. Visiting a new restaurant or going on a day trip to a place you've never been could be an easy way to do it.

Focus on having fun with each other. When a couple first starts dating, they are usually more easygoing and vibrant. But often this easygoing mindset can be forgotten when life's challenges start to get in the way or old grievances start to fester. Having a sense of humor indeed helps reduce stress, make tough situations easier to handle, and help in problem resolution. Think of simple ways to surprise your partner, like calling ahead to reserve a seat at their favorite restaurant or delivering flowers home. Playing with small children or dogs can also help you rediscover your fun side.

Work together on initiatives that will benefit others. One of the best ways to stay connected and close to your spouse is to emphasize something you both enjoy outside of the relationship. You may keep your relationship lively and meaningful by volunteering for a project, cause, or community service that you both find important. Additionally, it can present you both with the chance to network, learn from new perspectives, tackle novel challenges as a team, and create fresh channels of communication.

In addition to providing immense happiness, doing good things for others eases stress, anxiety, and sadness. People are naturally driven to want to help other people. The more you contribute, the better you'll feel as a team and as an individual.

Rekindle your conversation and mend your relationship. Ritual offers you tried-and-true interventions, helpful tools, and online therapy to help you improve your communication skills and repair and strengthen your relationships.

Tip 2: Keep in touch by communicating frequently.

Good communication is at the core of each healthy relationship. A strong emotional relationship between you and your partner makes you feel safe and happy. Individuals who lose their ability to relate also lose their ability to communicate, and times of stress or change can make this difference more noticeable. As long as you are communicating with each other, you can typically work out whatever problems you are having.

Tell your partner what you need instead of leaving them in the dark.
It's not always easy to communicate your needs. First of all, a lot of us don't think enough about our relationships or take the time to consider what's most important to us. Even if you are aware of your needs, talking about them could make you feel vulnerable, uneasy, or even shameful. But think about it from your partner's point of view. Offering comfort and understanding to someone you care about is a pleasure, not a responsibility.

If you've been dating for a while, you might think your partner knows you and your needs rather well. But your sweetheart isn't psychic. It is vital to express your desires clearly to avoid misunderstandings, even if your spouse seems to understand.

Even if your partner may detect something, you might not need it. Things that you needed and wanted five years ago might not be the same things that you need and want today because people evolve. Therefore, instead of letting anger, miscommunication, or resentment build when your partner frequently makes mistakes, make it a habit to tell them exactly what you expect from them.

Pay attention to the nonverbal cues your partner employs. We reveal so much about ourselves and our relationships through our silences. Spoken words do not transmit nearly as much information as nonverbal cues. These include how you stand, how you speak, how you make eye contact, and how you bend forward, cross your arms, or grip someone's hand.

Recognizing your partner's nonverbal cues, also referred to as "body language," can enable you to ascertain their genuine emotions and modify your response appropriately. For a relationship to work, both partners must be aware of their own and each other's nonverbal cues. There's a chance that your partner won't respond the same way as you. For example, one person might find that hugging someone after a difficult day is a kind way to communicate, but another person might rather take a walk or sit and talk.

Ensuring that your words and body language are consistent is also very important. If you declare to yourself, "I'm fine," but clench your teeth and look away, your body is telling you that you are anything but "fine".....

You feel happy and cherished when your partner gives you positive emotional cues, and you feel the same way when you offer them positive signs. If, especially during difficult times, you stop caring about your own or your partner's feelings, your relationship will suffer and your communication skills will decline.

Be mindful of your surroundings.
Even though communication is highly valued in our society, learning to listen in a way that makes someone feel heard and understood can help you build a deeper, more meaningful relationship with them.

Simple hearing is nothing like this type of listening. When you listen carefully and focus on what your partner is saying, you can read their actual feelings and the emotions they are trying to convey through small changes in their voice. Being a good listener does not need you to change your opinions or agree with your partner. On the other hand, it will help you find common ground that can help resolve conflicts.

Reduce your stress.
Stress and emotional exhaustion make it more likely that you may misread your romantic partner, give off ambiguous or disturbing nonverbal messages, or fall back

on risky routine habits. How many times have you become angry with a loved one and lost it, saying or doing something you later regretted?

By learning how to quickly release stress and return to a peaceful condition, you can avoid regrets like these as well as conflict and misunderstandings. When things get out of hand, you can even help your partner cool off.

Tip 3: Keep up your physical closeness

Touch is crucial to human existence. Studies conducted on infants have indicated the need for regular, affectionate touch for brain development. The benefits don't stop in childhood either. The hormone oxytocin, which is elevated in the body during loving touch, has an impact on bonding and attachment.

Sex is often the starting point of a committed relationship, but it shouldn't be the only way that two people get physically close. Touching someone frequently and lovingly—holding hands, embracing, kissing—is equally important.

Taking your partner's preferences into account is vital. . When the other person stiffens up and withdraws in reaction to unwanted touching or inappropriate advances, that's exactly what you don't want. Like so many other aspects of a great relationship, this can depend on how well you and your partner communicate your needs and aspirations.

Having regular couple time can help you retain physical closeness even with hard work or young children to look after. It can be as simple as setting aside an hour at the end of the day to sit and talk or hold hands.

Tip 4: In your relationship, practice giving and taking.

If you believe you will always get what you want in a relationship, you are setting yourself up for failure. Relationships that are compromised are the basis of health. Nonetheless, it takes work on the part of each person to guarantee a fair trade.

Take note of your partner's preferences.
Knowing what matters most to your partner will help you establish mutual respect and an atmosphere of compromise. On the other hand, you must let your spouse know what you want and that they get it. Altruism without self-preservation inevitably breeds resentment and fury.

Never let "winning" be your goal.
If you approach someone thinking you have to have your way or else, it will be difficult to reach a compromise. Having your wants not satisfied when you were younger or years of accumulating resentment in a relationship that has reached a breaking point can sometimes be the cause of this attitude. It's okay to have strong beliefs, but you should also give your partner a voice. Be mindful of other people's viewpoints.,

Understand how to resolve conflicts amicably.

Conflict may always arise in a relationship, but for it to last, everyone involved needs to feel heard. Not victory, but rather maintaining and strengthening the relationship, is the aim.

Make sure it's a fair fight. Honor the other person and keep your attention on the issue at hand. Don't start arguments over things that can't be changed.

Express your emotions through "I" statements as opposed to coming right out and attacking others. It could be better to say something like "I feel bad when you do that" rather than "You make me feel bad."

Avoid bringing up old arguments. Instead of placing blame on other people or focusing on past disagreements or complaints, think about what you can do to fix the problem right now.

possess the capacity to forgive. You will never be able to settle disputes if you are unable or unwilling to forgive others.

Move away from uncomfortable situations if they occur. Spend a few minutes relaxing and regaining your composure before saying or doing anything you'll later regret. Never lose sight of the fact that you and your beloved are at odds.

Know when enough is enough. If you can't agree, agree to disagree. It takes two people to continue a dispute. If a fight isn't going your way, you can decide to give up and go on.

Tip 5: Recognize that life will have ups and downs.

Recognize that there are highs and lows in any relationship.

You won't always agree, that much is true. Sometimes one partner is going through a difficult time, like the loss of a close family member. Relationships can become difficult as a result of several events, such as losing one's work or dealing with major health problems. You might view money management and childrearing from different angles.

Individuals react differently to stress, and misunderstandings can quickly turn into anger and irritation.

Never let your partner know how you're feeling. Life stress can make us lose our temper. When you're stressed, it could feel easier to vent to your partner and safer to snap at them. Although it might feel nice to fight like this at first, in the long run, it damages your relationship. Seek out constructive ways to release your stress, anger, and annoyance.

When trying to force a resolution, further problems could come up. Everyone has a different method for resolving disputes and issues. Remember that you are a team. You'll be able to get through the hard times by sticking together.

Think back to the early stages of your collaboration. Discuss the moments that first brought you together, think back to the times when you started to drift apart and decide how you two could work together to recreate that first passionate moment.

Remain receptive to new ideas. Change is inevitable in life and will happen whether you like it or not. Being adaptable is essential for strengthening the link in both happy and unpleasant times and for adjusting to the ongoing changes that take place in relationships.

Seek outside help together if your relationship calls for it. Sometimes relationship problems seem too difficult or complex for the two of you to handle on your own. Couples counseling and confiding in a trustworthy friend or a well-respected religious figure may also be helpful.

,

Chapter 3. Starting Our Self-Discovery Journey

A. Examining Individual Identity

Imagine a warm, engaging conversation by the fire where we actively listen as we share, fostering an environment that encourages openness and vulnerability. It's about delving deeper into the nuances that shape who we are, not just skimming the surface. What are the hopes, anxieties, and quirks that help to define who we are as people? These discussions take on the role of a mirror, displaying both our talents and our weaknesses. This sharing is not merely an admission of guilt; rather, it is the start of a shared understanding that establishes the groundwork for the new "we" we are becoming.

B. Matching Our Principles

Let's now discuss values, and the compass points that help us make decisions. What is dear to us? Which values direct our lives? This is a sincere examination of the values that speak to each of us individually; it is not a checklist. Envision developing a common moral code and a common GPS for our journey where our values complement each other. This is about discovering the symphony in the resonance of our ideals, not just about agreement. It's about creating a unified identity that transcends the sum of our separate identities.

Now grab a chair, and let's start these thought-provoking, humorous, and occasionally confrontational discussions. This self-discovery journey is not a lonely hike, but rather a tandem bike ride with lots of heart-to-hearts and twists and turns across the hills of understanding. We are creating something more than simply a friendship as we tell our tales, come together, and delve into the subtleties of who we are. It is a story that is uniquely 'us.' This is the core of our adventure together, my friend.

Chapter 4. Fostering Mutual Communication Proficiency

A.Promoting Free Communication

After defining our identities, let's take out the communication paintbrush and begin painting vivid pictures of understanding. Think of our discussions as a dynamic garden in which thoughts entwine, emotions ripple, and ideas grow. More than merely allowing ourselves to speak, encouraging open discourse involves providing a safe space where our thoughts can flow without fear of repercussions. It's the skill of being vulnerable with our ideas and emotions, creating an environment where our communication's sincerity serves as the foundation for our relationship to grow.

B. As a Team, Listening Actively

A vital part of this communication symphony is active listening. It involves training our senses to pick up on the nuances that lie just below the surface, not just listening to words. Let's listen to each other and not only respond in these exchanges; let's comprehend each other. Imagine it as a cooperative endeavor in which we both speak the spoken language. As we practice active listening together, it turns into a shared ability that we use to dance to the best of each other's stories, deepening our bond with each step.

C. Getting a Grip on Constructive Criticism

Not every communication is easy; occasionally, there are turbulences. To navigate these seas, one must accept constructive criticism as a guide for personal development. It's about offering helpful ideas and observations that guide us through difficult situations. Giving each other constructive criticism isn't the same as criticizing; rather, it's a cooperative instrument for improvement that helps us mold one other into our ideal selves.

Now, let's have a conversation in which we sit down together and use our words as paintbrushes to create a dynamic discussion that will ultimately create a masterpiece of connection. By encouraging candid communication and attentive listening, we build on our friendship and create the groundwork for a partnership that will grow and change with each discussion.

Chapter 5. Determining and Honoring Our Common Limits

A. Determining Our Combined Boundaries

By outlining some rules for our joint voyage, let's get started on the skill of traveling through life together. Consider this as creating a shared road map together in which we identify the areas that are specifically "yours," "mine," and the enchanted land that is "ours." Determining our shared boundaries isn't about erecting walls; rather, it's about establishing a haven where we can both feel appreciated, safe, and fully seen. This entails having an honest discussion about what makes us feel at ease, what is non-negotiable, and when we might need a little space to breathe. It's like drawing up a design for peaceful cohabitation, making sure that the "us" we are raising has a common ground for understanding and ideals to flourish on.

B. Respecting the Space of Others

The foundation of our joint journey is the respect of boundaries. It's the understanding that even if we're traveling together on this adventure, we're still two distinct people with unique goals, desires, and quirks. Respecting each other's personal space extends beyond physical bounds and includes understanding each other's emotional limits as well. It's about knowing when to assist and, just as importantly, when to permit yourself to grow. The magic of our relationship happens in this dance of juggling intimacy and independence, where "you" and "I" flow together to create the lovely song of "we."

C. Accepting Adaptability Within Our Boundaries

Let's accept that limits are just as fluid as the actual trip. Instead of being inflexible lines, they are dynamic landscapes that change as we do. Let us accept that our borders may change and evolve as we negotiate this common ground. This is evidence of our group's development and adaptation, not of instability. Being adaptable in our boundaries entails keeping a dialogue going about what suits us at various stages of our journey and acknowledging that our needs and wants may fluctuate. It's a pledge to always adjust our limits to ensure that they accurately represent who we are becoming and the growing bond between us.

Now, pour yourself a cup of virtual coffee, and let's work together to unravel this boundary map. Establishing and upholding our mutual boundaries is not about holding each other back; rather, it's about fostering a dynamic environment that supports our relationship and gives us the flexibility to explore, learn, and develop as individuals and as the exquisitely interwoven "we" that makes us who we are.

Chapter 6. Finding a Partner

Discovering a loving mate involves a deep investigation of compatibility, connection, and common goals. Imagine that 'you' and 'I' are setting out on a mission that transcends serendipity and random meetings within the wide terrain of relationships.

A. Comprehending Individual Values and Aspirations

Understanding oneself and one's values and desires is the first step toward finding a loving relationship. Imagine 'you' and 'I' as distinct people drawing a thorough map of our values, aspirations, and beliefs. It entails introspection—a quest to learn what matters most, what kindles passion, and what constitutes a satisfying relationship. By exploring this understanding, we establish a foundation for a relationship that is consistent with the fundamental principles that truly speak to 'us.'

B. Getting Around the Social Environment

Finding a romantic spouse requires purposeful social landscape navigation. Think of 'you' and 'I' as adventurers, exploring various social circles, participating in pursuits that suit our interests, and meeting people who have similar interests. It's an investigation that reaches behind the surface in search of ties based on sincere compatibility, common ideals, and a resonance that cuts through first impressions.

C. Establishing Valuable Relationships

It's important to focus on the quality of the relationships we create rather than the quantity when looking for a romantic companion. Making deep connections with people requires putting in the time and effort to get to know them better. Imagine 'you' and 'I' having meaningful discussions about feelings, dreams, and anxieties that go beyond mere talk. It's about fostering an atmosphere in which people feel comfortable enough to show vulnerability and where common experiences serve as the cornerstone of a deeper kind of connection.

D. Acknowledging Timing and Patience

The process of finding a loving companion requires timing and patience. Think of 'you' and 'I' as people who know that deep connections tend to happen on their own. It's about accepting the ups and downs of the trip, letting connections develop organically, and realizing that time is everything when it comes to a romantic relationship. When we are patient, we become the kind hand that tends to the potential seeds in each other's life, letting 'you' and 'I' blossom when the time is perfect.

E. Making Clear Intentions Communication

The key to converting contacts into possible love relationships is effective communication. Imagine 'you' and 'I' as communicators who authentically and ey their intents, wants, and expectations. 'You' and 'I' can share aspirations and dreams in an environment that fosters open communication, making sure that mutual understanding forms the cornerstone of a loving relationship.

F. Building an Intentional Relationship

Imagine 'you' and 'I' as intentional gardeners, carefully tending to the seeds of our relationship while a passionate connection blossoms. It involves devoting time and energy to creating a solid foundation, cultivating trust, and letting the relationship develop naturally. Building a space where love and friendship can develop, understanding each other's needs, and sharing experiences are all important aspects of nurturing a relationship.

See the complex process of finding a romantic partner as something that "you" and "I" are both involved in creating together—a journey that entails self-discovery, deliberate connection-building, patience, open communication, and the cultivation of a relationship with meaning. 'You' and 'I' join forces in this common journey not just as lovers but also as co-authors of a love tale that develops with nuance, significance, and the hope of a shared future.

Chapter 7. Our Devotion and How It Grows

Within the intricate fabric of our partnership, our dedication is not a fixed pledge but a dynamic, breathing organism that transforms and intensifies with time. Imagine 'you' and 'I' as the creators of a promise that transcends words and becomes a powerful force that bolsters and enhances the core of 'us.'

A. Laying the Groundwork for Trust

Our commitment is built on a foundation of trust, a holy place where "you" and "I" feel safe in the understanding and support we provide each other. Consider trust as the cornerstone of our commitment, a strong base that enables 'us' to withstand the storms and treasure the quiet times. It involves building a relationship based on trust that gets stronger with each shared experience by being dependable, truthful, and open.

B. Overcoming Obstacles Together

The furnace of adversity puts our dedication to the testt and solidifies it. Imagine 'you' and 'I' as lifelong friends traversing the ups and downs together. It entails putting up a united front in the face of difficulty and realizing that obstacles are only chances to show how committed we are. Our commitment grows as we overcome obstacles together and become stronger as a team via cooperative efforts, resiliency, and support from one another.

C. Fostering Sincere and Open Communication

Our commitment is centered on communication. Imagine 'you' and 'I' as communicators who value candor and transparency in our conversations. It entails paying attention to one another, sharing ideas and emotions without worrying about criticism, and fostering an environment where understanding is communicated through our words. Our relationship flourishes in the context of open communication, becoming richer and more profound as we continue to learn more about one another.

D. Joining Together to Celebrate Victories and Milestones

Our dedication is not only strengthened during trying times but also honored during victories and significant anniversaries. Envision 'you' and 'I' as accomplices in the happy moments that splatter along our path together. It is about celebrating one other's accomplishments, no matter how big or small, and taking pride in the common goals that add to the collective narrative of 'us.' Using these festivities, our dedication turns into a wellspring of mutual joy, strengthening the connection that binds "you" and "I."

E. Continuing to be Flexible and Sturdy

Our dedication changes throughout time with a built-in flexibility and toughness. Imagine 'you' and 'I' as partners who are strong and adaptable enough to ride the ever-changing waves of life. It entails changing with the times, picking up lessons from past mistakes, and developing both personally and as a pair. Our dedication transforms into a dynamic force in this dance of adaptability as we begin to comprehend that "you," "I," and "us" are always changing.

F. Fostering a Collective Future Vision

Imagining a future together, one that weaves "you" and "I" into a tapestry of hopes and desires, is essential to strengthening our bond. Imagine 'you' and 'I' as collaborators on this project, actively adding to the story of 'us.' It entails coordinating our respective objectives, supporting one another's dreams, and persistently pursuing a future that demonstrates profound action.

As 'you' and 'I' go through our commitment, picture it as an ongoing, dynamic adventure rather than a final destination. Throughout this journey, 'you,' 'I,' and the beautiful 'us' we continue to nurture and build become ever more committed to each other, and trust, resilience, open communication, shared celebrations, flexibility, and a shared vision become the pillars that maintain this commitment.

Chapter 8. Overcoming Obstacles as We Develop

As we make our way through its many turns, let's learn how to overcome obstacles as a team and reaffirm our strength as "us."

A. Handling Disagreements as a Combined Pair

Any trip will inevitably involve conflict, but the strength of our relationship is determined by how we resolve it as a team. Consider disagreements as chances for development rather than as obstacles. Open communication, attentive listening, and a shared dedication to problem-solving are necessary for resolving issues as a cohesive pair. It's about using setbacks as learning opportunities, growing as a team through every argument, and coming out on top.

B. Preserving Respect for One Another During Arguments

Let's cling to the principle of mutual respect even amid heated arguments. It's realizing that different points of view enhance rather than lessen the worth of our relationship. Respecting mutual regard entails accepting one another's viewpoints even when we disagree. It is an adherence to upholding the respectability of 'you' and 'I' in difficult situations, creating an atmosphere where our diversity enhances the breadth and depth of our common experiences.

C. Accepting Growth Despite Adversity

Obstacles are not barriers to overcome but rather opportunities for advancement. Adversity can be a catalyst for progress if one learns to see obstacles as chances for individual and group advancement. It's about working together to overcome obstacles, growing from them, and changing as we go. Our common approach to hardship serves as a stimulant for resilience, enhancing our bond and solidifying our knowledge that obstacles are opportunities for development rather than impediments.

When we take on obstacles, see it as a collaborative endeavor in which each setback leads to a common victory. Our journey becomes a monument to the power of our unity through disagreements, conflicts, and difficult times. Therefore, let's approach these difficulties not as enemies but as chances for development, understanding that each obstacle we overcome as a team fortifies the tie that unites "us."

Chapter 9. Maintaining Closeness and Emotional Connections

Let's immerse ourselves in the complex dance of maintaining intimacy as we travel through the landscapes of our shared trip. This is a magnificent symphony where romance, physical proximity, and vulnerability all come together to form the melody of our emotional relationships.

A. Admitting Our Weaknesses

Think of expressing our vulnerabilities as turning the pages of our books to disclose the most genuine chapters of our lives—our emotions. During these candid times, we develop a deep knowledge of one another. We shouldn't be afraid to share our dreams, worries, and anxieties since it's in this vulnerability that our emotional bonds are strengthened. By being vulnerable with one another, we create a place of trust where judgment is nonexistent and we may connect with the unadulterated beauty of our humanity.

B. Encouraging Romance in Our Bond

Love and admiration are the colors of romance, a kind of art that permeates every aspect of our everyday lives. It goes beyond making big gestures; it's about adding a little enchantment to the everyday. Together, let's explore the art of fostering romance via heartfelt gestures, surprising notes, and discovering joy in the everyday. The intentional acts of love, the shared laughter, and the snatched looks are what sustain the flame. Developing romance is about making every day an occasion to show each other how much we care and how much we appreciate each other, not just on special occasions.

C. Fostering Close Physical Bonds

Touch, proximity, and shared vulnerability are the choreography of physical intimacy, a dance that transcends the material. It's the warmth of hugs, the entwining of hands, and the unsaid language of physical intimacy. Embracing the emotional resonance that comes with physical closeness is just as important as the act of nurturing it. Let's delve into the depths of physical intimacy on this trip together, knowing that it is an expression of our emotional connection. It's about creating a space where touch speaks volumes and strengthens the bond between "you" and "I" in ways that words can never truly express.

Think of our connection as a garden, and maintaining closeness as giving the fragile flowers care. We strengthen the foundation of our emotional relationships by cultivating romance, dancing physical intimacy, and sharing vulnerabilities. This results in a tapestry that depicts our special and dynamic relationship. Thus, let us take good care of this garden, realizing that maintaining closeness is an ongoing process of love and learning rather than a destination.

Chapter 10. Parity and Collaboration within Our Union

Let's dive deeply into equality and cooperation in this revolutionary chapter of our shared story—a profound connection where "you" and "I" merge into the complex tapestry of "we."

A. Distributing Accountabilities

Imagine our partnership as a dynamic balance in which reciprocity becomes the dance of balancing duties. Divided work is not enough; we also need to realize that the journey we are on together is the load we bear. Recognizing the distinct abilities that each of us brings to the marriage and balancing the scales fairly and sensitively are essential components of this task. Our partnership's balance in this complex dance creates an atmosphere where both partners feel noticed, valued, and supported in their respective tasks.

B. Working Together to Make Decisions

Our path is a joint production, and the choices we make together are the brushstrokes in the masterwork. 'You' and 'I' become co-authors of our shared tale in collaborative decision-making, which is a complicated dance of ideas and viewpoints. It entails frank communication, attentive listening, and a dedication to identifying solutions that satisfy both parties. Our choices in this collaborative dance become more than just choices; they become a reflection of the strength and common vision that unites us.

C. Promoting Equitable Development

Imagine that both of us are the gardeners and the well-fed plants in a blooming partnership. Promoting mutual growth entails a continuous dedication to each other's advancement. Not only should individual accomplishments be acknowledged, but an atmosphere that allows both partners to grow and prosper should also be established. As a result of our mutual dedication to development, our partnership turns into a haven where the goals of "you" and "I" converge to produce a harmonious whole.

D. Accepting Differences in Roles

The distinctiveness of our roles is not eliminated by equality; rather, it is harmonized into a song that characterizes 'us.' Recognizing that each partner has a unique set of abilities, perspectives, and contributions is a necessary step in embracing the diversity of roles. It's about realizing the diversity of roles that enrich our union and how we, as a team, build a strong and vibrant collaboration. Our connection turns into a canvas in this dance of roles, where the colors of "you" and "I" meld together to become the vivid palette of "we."

Envision the concepts of equality and partnership as a dynamic symphony composed of harmony, cooperation, the development of both parties, and th,e celebration of various roles as we explore them. Our relationship in this common area develops into more than just a collaboration; it becomes a complex dance in which "you" and "I" grow, support, and change one another to create the lovely tapestry of "we."

Chapter 11. Accepting Our Continually Changing Partnership

As we embark on the significant phase of accepting the development of our partnership, picture it as a dynamic tapestry in which "you" and "I" are constantly weaving the threads that makeup "we."

A. Accepting Change as a Permanent

Life is full of change, and our relationship is no different. Think of our path as a river that is constantly changing as 'we,' our experiences, and growth all flow together. Accepting change as a given means being prepared to change, grow, and go through the ups and downs of our common story. It's about realizing that the only thing that is certain about our journey is that change is inevitable, and that acceptance gives us the fortitude to withstand any adversity.

B. Always Finding Each Other Again

Let's resolve to always discover more about each other as time passes. Think of our relationship as a book with countless chapters that are just waiting to be opened. It's about accepting the thrill of discovering new sides to "you" and "I" as we develop both personally and as a group. It is a deliberate act to keep finding each other again and again; it is a journey of inquiry, attentive listening, and sincere interest in the layers of our hearts that are always expanding.

C. Encouraging Common Dreams and Objectives

Our partnership is like brightly colored hopes and goals painted on a canvas. Fostering common dreams and objectives entails developing a shared vision of our future in addition to individual aspirations. It's about setting similar goals for ourselves, encouraging one another along the way, and commemorating the victories we share. As we work together to attain these shared goals, our relationship grows stronger and more inspiring, leading to more success and motivation.

D. Being Transparent About Expectations

The link between "you" and "I" in the ever-expanding "we" world is communication. Establishing a free-flowing environment where aspirations, goals, and future visions are expressed is essential to having an open conversation about expectations. It's about realizing that expectations might change and grow with time, necessitating ongoing communication to make sure both parties feel heard and understood. We establish the groundwork for a partnership that develops in step with our evolving needs in this candid conversation.

E. Working Together to Develop a Growth Mindset

Think of our relationship as a garden where intentional care is given to the seeds of growth. When we work together to cultivate a growth mindset, we see challenges not as barriers to overcome but as chances for mutual improvement. It's about creating an atmosphere in which each partner feels inspired to grow, develop, and become their best selves. Our partnership becomes a catalyst for both individual and group thriving as a result of our shared commitment to development.

Imagine our partnership as a dance as we go into the domain of accepting our constant change—a dance of transformation, rediscovery, shared dreams, honest communication, and a growth attitude. 'You' and 'I' thrive and flourish together in this sophisticated choreography, forming a lovely tale that celebrates the ongoing evolution of 'us.'

Chapter 12. Facing and Surmounting Obstacles Together

Let's examine the transforming process of facing and conquering hardships in this strong chapter of our journey—a cooperative effort in which "you" and "I" stand together against the storms that try the power of "us."

A. Taking On Challenges Head-On

Obstacles are not barriers; rather, they are the rough terrain that molds our relationship's topography. It takes a community's bravery to take on obstacles head-on and meet them head-on with unshakable commitment. Think of ourselves as a strong, united team, prepared to handle any challenge that comes our way. It's about seeing that obstacles are chances for development rather than weaknesses making them as a team, we strengthen the bonds that bind us.

B. Fostering Unity's Resilience

The foundation of our group's power is resilience. Think of our connection like a strong tree that stands firmly in its roots while swinging with the winds of misfortune. To build resilience in unity, people must weather adversity together with a common resolve to encourage and support one another. It's important to realize that hardship is an opportunity to show love on a deeper level rather than a sign that it is absent. By working together, we build a bond that gets stronger with each obstacle we face and become resilient architects.

C. Having Effective Conversations in Tough Times

We use communication as our anchor when the seas are choppy. Establishing a secure environment in which feelings, anxieties, and vulnerabilities can be shared without fear of rejection is essential to effective communication during trying times. It's about accepting that difficulties might elicit strong feelings in people and making a conscious effort to communicate openly to understand and support one another. Our ability to communicate at these times becomes essential for maintaining connection and reaffirming that "you" and "I" are in this together.

D. Seeking Encouragement and Support from One Another

Think of our collaboration as a shelter where the pillars that keep us upright during storms are our encouragement and support for one another. Recognizing that both spouses require strength and comfort during difficult times is a necessary step toward seeking mutual support. It's about reaching out to support one another when they stumble, giving supportive remarks, and fostering an environment where openness is greeted with understanding. "You" and "I" become each other's haven in this reciprocal act of support, strengthening the strong link that keeps "us" together.

E. Developing and Adapting to Difficulties

Adversities present chances for development rather than merely being impediments. Think of our relationship as a garden, where obstacles are the soil that helps us both grow. Resolving to draw lessons from trying circumstances is a necessary part of learning and developing from adversities. It's about growing both personally and as a group, seeing obstacles as opportunities to learn more about "you," "I," and the always changing "we" that we are all becoming.

Imagine 'you' and 'I' not just as partners but as strong allies navigating life's storms as you engage in this tenacious dance of facing and conquering obstacles. Collaboratively, we convert obstacles into learning opportunities, guaranteeing that each hardship encountered serves as evidence of the unwavering resilience and enduring affection that characterize 'us.'

Chapter 13. Growing Through All of Life's Stages Together

Let's explore the life-changing experience of evolving together through all the phases of life as we begin this new chapter of our journey—a shared evolution where "you" and "I" become entwined in the dynamic tapestry of "us."

A. Accepting Change as a Permanent

Seasons come into play in life, each bringing with it unique pleasures, difficulties, and changes. Accepting change as a given means realizing that life's stages are flexible and that our path is a never-ending story. 'You' and 'I' may be co-authors, guiding each other through the chapters of life. It involves embracing change with curiosity, resiliency, and a mutual resolve to adapt and prosper as a team.

B. Encouraging Personal Development

Individual development in our relationship garden results in the emergence of distinctive flowers inside the common ground. To foster individual growth, one must encourage the goals, objectives, and personal development of one another. It's about establishing a space where "you" and "I" develop personally and help "us" flourish as a group. Our relationship becomes a haven for personal thriving as we both commit to personal progress.

C. Rejoicing in Joint Milestones

Milestones are the moments of accomplishment, happiness, and celebration that dot the course of life. When we celebrate milestones together, we not only take pride in our accomplishments but also in the collective successes that help to build our story. It's about appreciating and honoring accomplishments of all sizes because they add to the patchwork of our common experiences. 'You' and 'I' become observers and contributors to the fabric of our shared experience during these joyous times.

D. Handling Difficulties in a Group

The shadows that accompany the sunlight of life's phases are called challenges. Managing obstacles as a group entails realizing that problems are shared duties rather than isolated burdens. It's about putting up a united front in the face of difficulty, providing steadfast support, and actively looking for solutions as a team. 'You' and 'I' become a powerful partnership during these trying times since we are both committed to overcoming setbacks and growing stronger.

E. Fostering Adaptability and Flexibility

The stages of life are erratic and necessitate adaptation and flexibility. Being flexible is being willing to adapt our course when the winds of change blow and bend without breaking. It's about having an open heart and being resilient enough to welcome life's unexpected turns. Our partnership becomes a vessel that skillfully navigates the constantly shifting currents of life in this dance of adaptability and flexibility, making sure that "you," "I," and "us" always remain in harmonious balance.

F. Savoring the Here and Now

The current moment, amid life's phases, is a valuable gem that has to be treasured. Cultivating attention, finding beauty in the mundane, and relishing the pleasures of the now is all part of cherishing the present. It's about living in the moment with "you" and "I," building a bank of recollections that strengthen the bonds between "us." Our partnership becomes a continuous celebration of the love and connection that characterize every moment as a result of this acceptance of the present.

Imagine 'you' and 'I' as dynamic players in a lovely dance of growth rather than as static entities as we grow together through the phases of our lifetime. As a team, we manage change, foster personal development, commemorate achievements, overcome obstacles, develop flexibility, and value the here and now. It's a journey that unites "you" and "me" into a resilient, dynamic "us."

Chapter 14 When Relationship Ends

The breakup of a partnership signifies a major turning point in the "you" and "I'm" shared journey. Even though ending a relationship can be difficult, it can also be a chance for introspection, healing, and personal development.

A. Recognizing Feelings

As this chapter of our partnership draws to an end, it's important to recognize the feelings that go along with this change. Imagine 'you' and 'I' as distinct people going through a range of emotions, such as sadness, loss, relief, or even a sense of release. It entails acknowledging that ending a relationship is a complicated and unique experience for both parties and giving ourselves permission to feel and process these feelings without passing judgme

B. Contemplating the Teachings Accrued

After a relationship ends, see 'you' and 'I' as introspective people who try to learn from the experiences that they have in common. It entails reflecting on the highs and lows, spotting trends, and drawing insightful conclusions that advance personal development. Thinking back on the lessons gained lays the groundwork for future healthy relationships and serves as a bridge to self-discovery.

C. Determining Limits

When the relationship ends, setting up boundaries become essential to getting through the post-breakup stage. Imagine that 'you' and 'I' are two people who freely discuss the need for personal space, time apart, and limits. By defining these boundaries, a more seamless transition can be ensured, enabling both parties to heal and proceed at their pace.

D. Making Self-Care a Priority

Imagine 'you' and 'I' as guardians of our health following the breakup. Setting aside time for self-care entails finding comfort in comfort-giving hobbies, asking friends or experts for help, and putting one's physical and mental well-being first. It's all about taking care of ourselves as individuals and realizing how important self-care is to the healing process.

E. Managing the Bereavement Process

Grieving at the end of a partnership is often similar to mourning the loss of a meaningful relationship. Imagine 'you' and 'I' as two distinct people going through this process together, with empathy and comprehension. It entails giving ourselves permission to grieve and accepting that healing is a process that takes time and progresses at its rate.

F. Asking for Help from Others

Imagine 'you' and 'I' with a network of friends, family, or colleagues who are all there to support you. Reaching out to people who can offer direction, empathy, and a listening ear the is the first step in seeking support. It's about realizing that getting well is a team effort and that drawing support from others may be an invaluable tool for overcoming the challenges of the post-break-up phase.

G. Acknowledging the Prospect of Development

As 'you' and 'I' work through the fallout from the breakup, consider the opportunity for personal development. It entails realizing that finding closure can present a chance for introspection, resiliency, and the pursuit of novel avenues. Releasing the potential for development enables 'you' and 'I' to proceed with enhanced understanding and a feeling of authority.

When our connection comes to an end, picture "you" and "me" as people traveling separately but crossing paths rather than as two distinct entities. Every path has the capacity to bring about healing, self-discovery, and the chance to rewrite our stories in ways that advance each person's development personal.

Chapter 15. Moving on

Exiting a relationship can be a difficult but necessary step on the path to self-awareness and personal development. Imagine 'you' as a person who can welcome fresh starts and 'I' as a collaborator on your path to recovery and rejuvenation.

A. Choosing to Accept

Imagine 'you' and 'I' as people who welcome acceptance as you move on. It entails accepting the fact that the relationship is over and realizing that it's an important milestone on the road to personal fulfillment. 'You' and 'I' can let go of attachments to the past and create space for the future when acceptance is the first step towards healing.

B. Recasting Viewpoints

Imagine 'you' and 'I' as reframers—people who deliberately change their viewpoint to highlight the advantages of the separation. It entails learning from mistakes, valuing one's development, and realizing that a relationship's dissolution may open doors to fresh experiences and chances. When it comes to negotiating the emotional terrain of moving on, reframing viewpoints becomes an effective tool.

C. Taking Part in Self-Revelation

Imagine yourself traveling on a trip of self-discovery as 'you' set out on the path of moving on. It entails rekindling personal interests, ambitions, and passions that may have been neglected during the relationship. "I" turns into an adventurer, actively searching for fresh aspects of one's personality and seizing the chance for development and personal fulfillment.

D. Setting Nutritious Limits

Think of 'you' and 'I' as boundary-setters—people who value self-care and set up sensible boundaries. It entails appreciating the emotional and physical need for space as well as upholding the boundaries that promote individual well-being. A crucial first step in moving on and laying the groundwork for future relationships is setting up healthy boundaries.

E. Fostering a Network of Support

Imagine 'you' surrounded by a network of friends, family, or professionals who will assist you as you go on. Building a support network entails asking for consolation and direction from people who are important to "you." "I" stands up, actively contributing to the healing process by being receptive to assistance and comprehension.

F. Making Use of Self-Compassion

Imagine self-compassion as a kind advisor while 'you' negotiate the challenges of moving on. 'I' becomes a source of self-compassion, offering understanding and care for oneself during periods of vulnerability. It entails treating oneself with respect, seeing that healing is a process, and realizing that it's okay to feel a range of emotions.

G. Accepting Fresh Starts

Imagine 'you' and 'I' as people prepared to welcome fresh starts. Relocating involves not only letting go but also becoming receptive to the opportunities that may come your way. It entails seeing a happy, expanding future with opportunities for satisfaction and making new connections. Accepting fresh starts turns into a celebration of bravery, resiliency, and the changing "you" and "I."

See the process of moving on as a transformational weave in which "you" and "I" become the creators of our own stories. It's a voyage of self-awareness, self-compassion, and a proactive search for a happy and fulfilled future.

94

Chapter 16. When Someone Ends Their Relationship With You

A person leaving you can cause a wide range of feelings as well as a major change in your life. Imagine 'you' as a person negotiating the intricacies of this experience, and 'I' as your inner fortitude and resiliency that supports you during it.

A. Recognizing Feelings

As it happens, imagine 'you' admitting a range of feelings. It entails permitting yourself to experience any arising emotions, including sadness and loss. "I" emerges as the sympathetic inner partner who understands that expressing feelings is an essential first step toward recovery.

B. Making a Healing Environment

Imagine 'you' actively making room for recovery. It entails allowing yourself to mourn and adjust to the changes. 'I' take on the role of the nurturer, supporting your self-care throughout this transitional phase and attending to your emotional health.

C. Looking for Assistance

During the departure, imagine 'you' reaching out for assistance. Seeking support—from experts, friends, or family—becomes essential to the recovery process. "I" takes on the role of the advocate, seeing the value of relating to people through trying times and the power that comes from being vulnerable.

D. Examining One's Own Development

Imagine 'you' looking back on your personal development as time goes on. The move presents a chance for personal growth and self-discovery. "I" takes on the role of the spectator, realizing the strength and resiliency that come from taking on obstacles and accepting change.

E. Developing Hardiness

Imagine 'you' developing resilience after someone leaves. It entails adjusting to the changes, drawing lessons from the encounter, and growing stronger as a result. "I" take on the role of the resilience architect, assisting you on your path to overcome hardship.

F. Putting Self-Care First

Imagine 'you' making self-care a priority during this shift. It entails taking part in activities that uplift and cheer you up while nourishing your mental and physical health. I take on the role of caregiver, advising you on the value of practicing self-compassion and making time for self-care.

G. Accepting Fresh Starts

Picture 'you' accepting the idea of fresh starts as the departure signifies an end. It entails anticipating the opportunities that lie ahead. I take on the role of the optimist, pointing the way for you toward a future rich in development, opportunity, and the chance to make new friends and encounters.

Imagine someone's journey away from you not as a conclusion to a story, but as a new chapter in the greater story of 'you.' 'I' becomes the constant, helping you navigate the waves of change and pointing the way toward a future where self-discovery, resiliency, and fresh starts are all interwoven into the fabric of your ever-changing journey.

Conclusion

Our investigation of relationships has woven across the vast symphony of love, grief, and the complex dance of 'you' and 'I.' It is crucial that we consider the connections we have made, the feelings we have discovered, and the transforming potential ingrained in our common connection trip as we stand at the end of this deep expedition.

This investigation delves deeply into the fundamentals of human connection rather than just analyzing interpersonal dynamics. Similar to the tides, relationships are dynamic and fluid, always changing things that are fashioned by the interactions between partners' tenacious spirits, understanding, and emotions.

As was previously mentioned, the echoes of departure represent both the close of one chapter and the start of a new one that will bring about transformation. Comparably, the study of relationships denotes more than merely a glimpse into the intricacies of bonding; it's a recognition of the enormous influence that "you" and "I" have on one another's life. We Ve experienced highs and lows together, seen the beauty in vulnerability, and welcome the development that comes from life's common experiences.

Our shared experience highlights the significance of resilience, communication, and understanding as the cornerstones of a healthy relationship in the great orchestration of emotions. Together, 'you' and 'I' are dynamic forces rather than static objects, co-authors of a story that is shaped by every moment spent together, every victory, and every obstacle overcome.

Imagine this exploration's conclusion as a pause, not its end—a chance to consider, assimilate, and apply the lessons discovered. In their flexibility, relationships offer us chances for personal development, self-awareness, and the ongoing improvement of the "you" and "I" connection.

Allow this investigation to serve as a catalyst for 'you' to actively participate in the continuum conversation about 'us.' It's a call to embrace honest communication, find beauty in vulnerability, and develop the resilient spirit that keeps partnerships strong through all the shifting phases of life.

May the echoes of this investigation stay as a reminder that the trip is just as important as the destination in the vast symphony of "you" and "I," where departures are but transitions and connections are ever-evolving. Let 'you' and 'I' move on together, writing the next chapters with purpose, empathy, and a mutual dedication to the flourishing story of 'us.'